Katie -

I hope you get to explore all of Oregon. It's a beautiful state and a great place to live.

Welcome -

Mary

Beautiful America's
Oregon

Beautiful America's

Oregon

By Charlotte Dixon

Beautiful America Publishing Company

Front cover: Beautiful Mt. Hood from Trillium Lake

Opposite title page: Heceta Head Lighthouse (1894)

Published by
Beautiful America Publishing Company
P.O. Box 244
Woodburn, OR 97071

Library of Congress Catalog Number 2007019679

ISBN 978-0-89802-863-8
ISBN 978-0-89802-862-1 (paperback)

Printed in Korea

Contents

Portland Skyline and Hawthorne Bridge

International Rose Test Gardens, Washington Park

The Flower Festival comes to Pioneer Courthouse Square

Introduction

Ah, Oregon--the name alone conjures images of exploration, adventure and quirky individualism. And with good reason — this western state (the 33rd to enter the Union) with its varied terrain, has long been an outpost for dreamers. Perhaps it is the sheer variety you can find here. Longing for wild waves and booming surf? Oregon's 362 miles of beach (every last inch of it public) will surely fill the bill. How about some amazing powder skiing, snowshoeing or just playing in the snow? Mt. Hood, Mt. Bachelor, and other Cascade peaks beckon. Perhaps an urban experience is more to your liking? Visit Portland, with its well-deserved reputation for fine dining and innovative restaurants, and feast on local favorites such as salmon and hazelnuts. And don't forget the state's reputation as a producer of fine wines and hearty beers. You'll find culture in the form of world-class theater, music and ballet. Yet, if you long for vast vistas and stretches of empty land, only a few hours drive will land you in the high desert of eastern Oregon.

Begin your visit by learning how to say the name correctly, as the locals are very particular about this. It is pronounced Or-uh-gun, please not, Or-ee-gone. Saying it the latter way will brand you as an outsider immediately. Oregonians are proud of their gorgeous state, beginning with the name.

Perhaps some of this pride stems from the state's unique history. Oregon was originally settled by steely visionaries who crossed the Oregon Trail by wagon train, and many descendants of these courageous pioneers still live in the state. You'll find fascinating Oregon Trail historical sites across the state, and in some areas you can still see the deep ruts carved by wagon wheels. There's also a strong Native American presence in Oregon, with tribe-run casinos thriving and many Indian names given to geographic features.

But newcomers make up a huge portion of the population. Seeking the laid-back outdoor lifestyle that Oregon offers, many residents emigrated from more populous areas to the south or east and wouldn't return to their old lives for the world—rain notwithstanding! Many years ago, Oregon's beloved governor, Tom McCall, made news when he exhorted tourists to visit but not stay. Though the state is much more welcoming to newcomers than such a comment might imply, the spirit of Tom McCall lives on in a rabid love of the environment. You'll get shocked, disdainful looks if you throw away a glass bottle or aluminum can. Oregon is a state of careful recyclers. After all, it is the home of the bottle bill, the first state to require that bottles and cans be returnable, and recently expanded to include plastic water bottles.

Nestled next to the Pacific Ocean, and bordered by the states of Washington, Idaho, Nevada, and California, Oregon covers 97,073 square miles of contrasts. From field to canyon, raging river to quiet lake, snow-capped mountain to rugged coast, green valley to sophisticated urban areas, there's something for everyone to enjoy in this state. So sit back, relax, and enjoy your tour of Oregon.

Portland

We'll begin our tour in Portland, the largest city in Oregon with a population of two million people, and the first glimpse many visitors have of the state. Drawn by the city's reputation for fine cuisine, bustling microbrewery scene and arty vibes, many tourists fly into Portland's international airport to start their Oregon vacation. Located at the northern edge of the state, Portland lies near the confluence of the Willamette and Columbia rivers. The Columbia forms the state's border with the state of Washington, its northern neighbor. The Willamette neatly divides the city into east side and west side, and provides a convenient landmark by which to navigate—to say nothing of a variety of water-based activities.

Visitors to Portland never need to worry about getting around—the city is known as a pioneer in transportation. Portland is a town of green-minded citizens, and this is reflected in its transportation. Over 3.5 percent of the city's workers commuted by bike in 2005, and this number only continues to grow. Less hardy souls commute via public transportation. As a visitor, you can, too.

Fall comes to the Japanese Garden, Washington Park

Opposite page: Portland Classical Chinese Garden

Take light rail (called MAX by the locals, for Metropolitan Area Express), ride a bus, or hop on the street car which runs throughout downtown. Information is easy to find on the transit authority's website. The city is highly walkable, too, and several companies offer walking tours of historical or scenic interest.

However you get around, come prepared with a variety of clothing. As the locals will tell you, there's no place like the Northwest in the spring, but temperatures are variable and can range from highs in the eighties to lows in the forties. Portland shares a marine climate with the rest of the western portion of Oregon, and as such the summers are warm and dry but the winters tend to be cool and rainy. This is an ideal climate for gardening, and Portland is known as a perfect spot for growing roses, which is how it got its nickname, the City of Roses. Every June the city celebrates its beloved flower with the Rose Festival, which includes three parades, a band competition, queen coronation, and fun center along the riverfront.

The city's love of roses is on display at the International Rose Test Gardens in Washington Park, which features 7,000 rose bushes of over 550 varieties. Spend a pleasant afternoon strolling the gardens, and then head over to visit the Pittock Mansion. Be sure to note the stunning views of the city with Mt. Hood in the background. While in the neighborhood, you must visit our Oregon Zoo, one of the finest in the country. From here, it's a quick hop up to the Japanese Gardens, also a part of Washington Park. Other public gardens of note include the fairly new Portland Classical Chinese Garden in Old Town and the Crystal Springs Rhododendron Garden on the east side of town. You'll also notice that Portland is a city of parks. Visit the 5,000-acre Forest Park, one of the largest urban wilderness areas in the United States, and Tom McCall Waterfront Park, home to many festivals and fairs throughout the year.

Are you now in the mood for some urban atmosphere? Portland features a variety of neighborhoods that are fun to wander through. There's downtown, with its department stores, boutiques, coffee shops (a fixture in every neighborhood), and restaurants. You won't want to miss Pioneer

Courthouse Square, known as "Portland's Living Room," which is located smack dab in the middle of town and host to concerts, movie nights, rallies, blossom festivals, brew fests, and a Christmas tree-lighting ceremony every year on the day after Thanksgiving. Portlanders love their civic events!

Two other neighborhoods of note border downtown. Old Town lies near the river and is home to the Saturday Market, a Portland tradition of long standing. Here, vendors gather every weekend between April and December to sell handmade goods. Further west is the Pearl District, an area of lofts, art galleries and trendy restaurants. First Thursday is held every month by the Pearl's art galleries to feature the openings of new shows.

No tour of Portland is complete without a visit to the east side, dominated by comfortable old residential neighborhoods, major malls (Lloyd Center, the oldest shopping mall in the country, and Clackamas Town Center), and charming shopping districts. Other fun neighborhoods to wander are the Hawthorne District, Hollywood, and the burgeoning International District located around Sandy Boulevard, where many Vietnamese restaurants, bars, and groceries thrive.

If you happen to hit town on a rainy day, never fear—there are many museums and cultural institutions to visit. Try the Oregon Historical Society on the Park Blocks for a dose of the state's history; or, if you're in the mood for science, hit OMSI, the Oregon Museum of Science and Industry. The Portland Art Museum features many blockbuster exhibits and lovers of culture and nightlife will find a vibrant theater and music scene here, as well as opera. When you've had your fill of culture, you can choose a book from Powell's, fondly called the City of Books, the largest bookstore in the world, and peruse it while sipping a beer from one of the many microbrews which make their home in Portland.

Alas, it is time to cut our visit to Portland short. But never fear, because many more delights await in our tour of this beautiful state.

Pittock Mansion in Portland

Come visit our fabulous Oregon Zoo

Rose Festival Carnival Night on Portland waterfront

Harbor and Astoria-Megler Bridge

Astoria Column

Oregon Coast

Our next destination is the stunning Oregon Coast, a vast shoreline of rugged rock formations, beautiful beaches, and crashing surf that runs 362 miles from its northern border with Washington to the southern border that abuts California. Every single inch of those beaches are open to the public with free beach access to all, thanks to a revolutionary bill passed in 1967.

The Oregon coast is often divided into three distinct areas—the north coast, from the Columbia River to the town of Neskowin; the central coast, from bustling Lincoln City to the sand dunes of Florence; and the south coast, running from Reedsport all the way to the California-Oregon border. Each of these coastal regions features unique local history and flora and fauna, including a wide array of charming towns and even some fairly big cities.

Let's begin our tour on the north coast, at the far northwestern tip of Oregon. Located a short, pleasant drive of just under a hundred miles from Portland, is the picturesque city of Astoria. This town of nearly 10,000 people has been the setting for many movies, including *Free Willy*, *Kindergarten Cop*, and *The Goonies*, and it is easy to see why. Lovely Victorian homes march up hills overlooking the Columbia River and the Pacific, just a couple miles away. Stroll the city's historic waterfronts or stop for lunch at a café overlooking the river and watch gulls dive for their meal. Astoria is the oldest settlement west of the Rocky Mountains, and throughout the 1800s it was known for its rich fur trading and salmon harvest. Capture a bit of this history by visiting the Columbia River Maritime Museum, which honors the town's seafaring tradition; or the Flavel House Museum, which will give you a unique viewpoint into how the wealthy of a different era lived. You'll also want to stop at the Astoria Column, standing 125 feet tall atop Coxcomb Hill, which overlooks the city. Views from the top can't be beat.

Heading south down the coast, the hardy among you might want to consider camping at Fort Stevens State Park. Of great interest to the history buff will be Fort Clatsop, the site of the winter encampment of the Lewis and Clark Corps of Discovery in 1805-1806. This park features an interpretive

Cannon Beach from Ecola State Park

center and a replica of the fort itself, the original of which had rotted away by the 1880s. It's easy to see why Lewis and Clark complained about the incessant rain here—this area gets 70 inches of rain a year.

Take a break from history and come back to the glorious present, heading south to the coastal resort towns of Gearhart and Seaside, the latter of which has been a Spring Break destination for legions of Oregon teenagers. The long beach here is bordered by the Prom, a two-mile walkway built in the 1920s. Seaside features many cute shops, a variety of stores selling fudge, cotton candy, and other delights, a game arcade, and a miniature fairway as well. And to top it all off—there's even a carousel to ride while enjoying your stash of treats.

Highway 101 is the road which will take you all the way from border to border, and we'll hop back on it now and head into Cannon Beach, just a short drive away. Cannon Beach is an artsy community which takes its name from a cannon that washed ashore from the USS Shark in 1846. You won't find any fast-food restaurants or strip malls here—the city's charter won't allow it. Instead, enjoy kite shops, boutiques, and pizza parlors situated in lovely wood buildings, some old, some new. Many Portlanders visit this part of the coast to engage in a favorite Oregon activity—whale watching. The best months to spot these giant mammals are December, March, and August. You'll find volunteers staffing spots at Ecola State Park and Neahkahnie Mountain, as well as other spots along the coast. You'll find them standing near the "Whale Watching Spoken Here" signs. While looking for whales, be sure to see the Cannon Beach landmark of Haystack Rock, the third-largest rock monolith in the world. It's a bird sanctuary and a great spot to bird watch.

Charming towns abound along the Oregon Coast, and we'll pass through several of them immediately south of Cannon Beach. There's Manzanita, Nehalem, and Wheeler, triplets bordering Nehalem Bay. Further on we reach serious deep-sea fishing country, with the small port town of Garibaldi, which is famous both for its fishing fleet and excellent clamming. History buffs will slam on the brakes for a stop at the Garibaldi Museum, which tells the story of Robert Gray, who discovered the Columbia River in 1792. (In case you are curious why the river is not named the Gray River, it is because he named it after his ship.)

This part of the coast is also dairy country, with the famed Tillamook herds located here. Locals will tell you there's no better ice cream or cheese than that made with love by Tillamook, and you can get a taste of it yourself with a visit to the Tillamook Cheese Factory. The self-guided tour features an observation area where you can watch the fascinating cheese-making process for yourself. And don't forget the free cheese samples and a visit to the gift store, where you can buy a variety of products to take home with you.

The one detour we'll take off Highway 101 is a good one, for it will lead us along the Three Capes Scenic Loop, where you'll see Cape Meares, Cape Lookout, and Cape Kiwanda. And now, returning to 101, we'll begin our exploration of the central coast. One of the most beloved vacation spots for Oregonians is Lincoln City, a bustling beachside town which offers a variety of delights, from strolling the seven miles of beach to fine dining and shopping. One thing you'll notice if you're into beachcombing is the preponderance of kites. The winds here are excellent for kite flying, and aficionados flock here to experience the activity. Lincoln City is so well known for this, that it has been named the Kite Capital of the World, and it celebrates this distinction with kite festivals in May and September. And for those of you who prefer your fun indoors, you'll find the Chinook Winds Casino Resort perfect for a visit.

Further south is Depoe Bay, a fairy-tale fishing village where you can shop and dine with spectacular ocean views, thanks to a seawall that runs along the town's entire length. You'll also want to keep an eye out as fishing boats negotiate their way out to sea, as Depoe Bay boasts the world's smallest navigable harbor as part of its charms. And by the way, you can charter one of those fishing boats yourself, or sign on for a whale-watching tour.

Next up is Newport, a picturesque town situated between the Coast Mountains, the Pacific Ocean, and Yaquina Bay. Visit the historic Nye Beach area and stay at the Sylvia Beach Hotel, where rooms are decorated to honor

The "Needles" at sunset, Cannon Beach

Manzanita from Neahkahnie Mountain

famous authors. And don't forget to spend time at the Bayfront, the traditional fishing and timber center that now features shops, restaurants and even attractions such as the Ripley's Believe It or Not Museum. And whatever you do, don't miss a visit to the Oregon Coast Aquarium, once the home of Keiko, of the movie *Free Willy* fame.

We'll pass through Waldport and Yachats as we continue south, and take a look at the Heceta Head Lighthouse, before stopping at Sea Lion Caves. This natural cave is home to a huge herd of sea lions, which you can see by taking stairs and an elevator down to a viewing area. Our final stop on the Central Coast is Florence, which is known as a great place to retire, among other things. This town is full of historical significance, and you can learn about that at the Siuslaw Pioneer Museum. You'll also want to save time for a stop at the Jessie M. Honeyman Memorial State Park, where you can explore miles of sand dunes, camp overnight and enjoy water sports on the park's three lakes.

Now it's onto the South Coast, where Reedsport and its neighbor, Winchester Bay, like to call themselves the "Heart of the Oregon Dunes." Next we'll find the cities of Coos Bay, North Bend, and Charleston, which together are known as the Bay Area, and all of which offer shopping, dining, and many other amenities. Further south, Bandon is known as the Cranberry Capital of Oregon, and you'll see many bogs as you drive along Highway 101. These bogs grow 30 million pounds of berries every year.

Port Orford and Gold Beach are next, both of which are popular with retirees. Finally, the town of Brookings-Harbor is our last stop on our coastal tour. This lovely city is the banana belt of the coast, with temperatures routinely reaching 70 to 80 degrees. You can see why it is also a popular retirement spot.

Regretfully, it is time to turn our backs on the ocean and head inland, as we discover all the delights that southern Oregon has to offer.

Southern Oregon

Southern Oregon is filled with enchantments for the tourist, from rugged outdoor adventures to cultural treats, including world-class theater. The first stop on our southern Oregon tour is a visit to the historic Oregon Caves. This national monument nestled in the Siskiyou Mountains is a 488-acre park known for its marble caves. The cave was discovered in 1874 by Elijah Davidson, when his dog Bruno chased a bear into a cave. Davidson found easy entry, but a bit tougher exit, as it took him and Bruno seven hours to find their way out! Shortly thereafter the caves became an attraction that was soon opened as a commercial enterprise.

Now operated by the National Park Service, the Caves are a favorite destination. You'll want to take one of several tours offered in order to see the majestic caves. However, be forewarned that the cave tours are considered to be moderately strenuous, and they most definitely are not recommended for people who have difficulty walking, or who have heart or breathing problems. The half-mile route features more than 500 stairs and there are some low passageways you'll need to duck through. Children must have reached a height of 42 inches or more and demonstrate that they can climb stairs in order to take the tour. Visitors of all ages are encouraged to dress warmly, as the caves are 44 degrees year-round. (For purposes of comparison, that's the temperature of your refrigerator—brrrrr.)

Once you've taken your cave tour, extend your visit with a stay at the rustic Oregon Caves Chateau. A National Historic Landmark, this six-story hotel sports 23 guest rooms, as well as a dining room and coffee shop. It is generally open from early May through October. Because the caves are in a gorgeous wilderness area, you'll find much to do nearby, including wine tasting at two nearby wineries, and fantastic hiking.

Now let's head north and west to take in the delights of Grants Pass. Situated on the "Wild and Scenic" Rogue River, Grants Pass has a welcoming, small-town feel to it. From downtown docks, jet boats leave for a variety of Rogue River tours. There's also plenty of whitewater rafting nearby, as well

Boiler Bay between Lincoln City and Newport

Opposite page: "The World's Smallest Harbor," Depoe Bay

as kayak rentals and rafting tours. Grants Pass is a city that loves its river and its water activities! But there's also much more to this place, including a National Historic District that features turn-of-the-century architectural gems, now housing shops, restaurants, and galleries. You may want to time your visit to one of the many fairs and festivals that the city hosts. How about the Amazing May Celebration? This festival is held in, you guessed it, May, and features a dog show, a wine stroll, an antique street fair, and a hot-air balloon festival. Or how about Art Along the Rogue, a painting festival held every October? Or maybe you'd prefer Back to the Fifties, an event in July that attracts classic car enthusiasts from all over the country.

For those of you who enjoy scenic drives, try the Rogue River Loop, a twenty-mile-long excursion into history. You'll enjoy visiting the Applegate Trail Interpretive Center, which tells the story of this famous southern portion of the Oregon Trail. At the center you'll see exhibits dedicated to the first pioneer settlers, the discovery of gold in the area, and the subsequent building of the railroads. There's also an authentic covered wagon and nearby is the Graves Covered Bridge. Further along on the Loop, stop in at the Wolf Creek Inn, once known as the Wolf Creek Tavern, an historic stage coach lodge which to this day offers fine dining and lodging. The Loop area also includes the ghost town of Golden, the river town of Galice, and numerous gold mines, leftovers from the boom.

Now we're going to head south again, stopping first in Medford, a city of over 77,000 people, with a metropolitan population of over 200,000. The wine connoisseur will be in heaven here, as the Medford area is home to a growing number of wineries and vineyards. There are also plenty of artisan cheeses and specialty chocolates available in the beautiful rolling hills that surround this town. Medford features an historic downtown district, where you'll discover restaurants, shops, galleries and taverns aplenty. One not-to-be-missed stop is Harry and David, the world-renowned gourmet mail-order company. Not only are the company's headquarters here in town, you can also visit their Country Village in order to shop for all kinds of goodies. Don't forget to pick up some luscious pears, the company's specialty.

South of Medford is the charming town of Ashland, which lies at the southern tip of the Umpqua Valley, almost to the border of California. Ashland is the home of Southern Oregon University, and the Oregon Shakespeare Festival, both of which add a debonair aura to the town of nearly 20,000. Ashland offers so many delights it is hard to know where to begin. Outstanding restaurants and beautiful bed and breakfast locations abound. Indeed, numerous magazines have named it one of the best small towns in America.

Perhaps it is because of the city's broad boulevards, curvy streets running up the hillside behind the town, or the gorgeous 100-acre Lithia Park, which features a pond with live swans, and world-famous Lithia water. Try it at one of the water fountains in the park—it's a memorable experience. This mineral water has quite a strong taste and a bit of effervescence and urging new visitors to taste it is a favorite sport among the locals.

But Ashland is best known for the Oregon Shakespeare Festival, which has an international reputation. Indeed, visitors come from all over the world to attend the plays. The festival sells more tickets to more plays than any other theater in the country, and in an average year, 350,000 tickets are sold, with 100,000 visitors attending plays. The festival features three stages, including the outdoor Aiken Pavilion or Elizabethan Stage, the indoor Angus Bowmer, and the new theater. The season runs from February through October and you'll see a variety of plays offered, with many contemporary and historic plays presented. The Oregon Shakespeare Festival is one of the few theater companies committed to presenting all of Shakespeare's plays, even the less regularly presented ones such as the history plays. Be sure to get to events at the outdoor theater early, as you'll be treated to a "Green Show," which may feature Elizabethan music, dance performances, clown acts, jugglers or any number of other acts!

Skiers may want to take a break from the city to try out the slopes at the Mt. Ashland ski area, just 18 miles south of town. You'll also want to investigate some of the festivals the town hosts, including a spectacular Old Fashioned Fourth of July celebration, complete with fireworks, and the December Festival of Lights, and Santa's Parade during the winter holidays.

Heceta Beach looking south towards Florence

Oregon Dunes National Recreation Area

Cape Arago Lighthouse, Charleston

It is difficult to pull ourselves away from Ashland, but fortunately, the delights of another nearby small town await. The gold rush town of Jacksonville is nestled among historic orchards and vineyards and features 85 historic buildings, many of them now sporting charming shops and cafes. You may do a double take upon first glimpse of the town's main street, because it looks like the set of a western movie. So it will come as no surprise that it has been in quite a few films.

One of the town's best-loved traditions is the annual Britt Festival, a concert series held each summer in an open-air amphitheater, which is nestled beneath a hill that forms natural acoustics. You'll experience all kinds of music at the Britt Festival, including pop, alternative, country and classical.

Leaving Jacksonville, we're going to climb into the high country of southern Oregon, with a vast array of outdoor opportunities, including lakes and mountains offering fishing, sailing, kayaking, camping, canoeing and just plain old-fashioned exploring. The centerpiece of the Klamath County outdoor experience is the magnificent Crater Lake National Park. This is Oregon's only national park, and a deserving location for it. Crater Lake is a caldera lake of stunning beauty, thanks to its deep blue color. The deepest lake in the United States at 1,932 feet deep, it was formed over 5,000 years ago with the collapse of the volcanic Mt. Mazama.

The lake has spiritual significance beyond its beauty. The local Klamath Tribe Indians have long regarded it as a sacred site, with ancestors of long ago likely witnessing the eruption that formed the lake, which is alluded to in their legends. The tribe often uses the lake as a site for vision quests. One interesting note about Crater Lake—because it has no tributaries, it has some of the purest water around.

Visitors may want to take a night to stay at the Crater Lake Lodge, located on the rim of the lake and run by the National Park Service. The lodge was begun in 1909 and designed to carry an especially heavy snow load for eight months of the year, since the lake averages 533 inches of snowfall. During your stay, be sure to take a boat tour of the lake, from which you can view Wizard Island in the center of the lake, and The Old Man of the Lake, a tall tree stump which has been bobbing in the water for over one-hundred years. Another favorite activity is driving or cycling Rim Drive, which circles the lake.

From Crater Lake, we travel on to the business and commercial center of the high country of southern Oregon—the city of Klamath Falls. It is the county seat of Klamath County and has a population of around 20,000. Besides an historic city center which you can experience through walking tours, the city also has many outdoor activities. You may want to play golf at the Running Y Ranch Resort, which boasts a course designed by Arnold Palmer. The Klamath Falls area is a bird watcher's dream because of its location on the Pacific Flyway. You'll see lots of raptors and waterfowl year round. Look for the American White Pelican and the Bald Eagle, large numbers of which are concentrated in Bear Valley, a few miles south of town.

Now we're going to head north again. We've got a couple more stops on our tour of southern Oregon, premier among them the town of Roseburg. The county seat of Douglas County, and home to approximately 20,000 people, Roseburg features an historic downtown and easy access to both the North and South branches of the Umpqua River. Hike along riverside trails and view waterfalls, fish for salmon and steelhead, or the more daring may want to experience whitewater rafting. Visit the Douglas County Museum, a few miles south of town, for wonderful displays of natural (and human!) history.

No visit to the area is complete without a stop at the Wildlife Safari, located in Winston. Drive through the park and view over 500 animals roaming free in their natural habitats. Wildlife Safari is much more than just a tourist destination, however. It is a nationally accredited zoological preserve which is dedicated to conservation, education, and research. One of the cornerstones of the park's mission is its cheetah-breeding program, which began in 1973, a year after the park was founded. Since then, 38 litters and 149 cheetahs have been born at the park. Cubs from the park now live in zoos across the country. Wildlife Safari is also active in preserving rare and endangered species around the world. You'll find many opportunities to get up close and

Beautiful Shore Acres State Park near Coos Bay

personal with the animals at the park, including the Elephant Carwash, Camel Rides, photos with Taini, the ambassador Cheetah, and the Safari Petting Zoo. There is also a lion area, and a bear area, (but only when they come out of hibernation in the spring.)

Yes, the delights of southern Oregon are profuse indeed. But as we leave Wildlife Safari we'll be waving goodbye to this part of the state for now. Odds are good you'll be returning soon, however, with all that the region has to offer. Now we turn to another part of the state, the Willamette Valley.

Willamette Valley

The Willamette Valley is the lush agricultural land that surrounds the Willamette River, a river unique for the fact that it flows north, eventually emptying into the grand Columbia. And let's get one thing straight from the start—the valley and the river are pronounced Will-AM-it. A favorite destination of pioneers laboring over the Oregon Trail, the valley today is home to two vibrant college towns, the state capital, over 200 wineries, and a variety of cultural and outdoor activities. Bounded on the west by the Coast Range Mountains and the east by the Cascades, the valley is a fertile mecca for modern-day visitors.

We'll start our tour in the city of Eugene, known as the home of the University of Oregon, the grand dame of the state's higher-education system. Situated at the southern end of the Willamette River, Eugene is the second-largest city in Oregon with a population of 154,650. It is also known for quirkier reasons, such as activist politics, alternative lifestyles, and a general laid-back air.

The city is sometimes referred to as "Track Town" because of the university's dominance in track and because Nike had its start here. Legendary Bill Bowerman, who invented the famous sport-shoe company's waffle soles on his wife's waffle iron, coached track at the U of O for 24 years. One of his most famous athletes was Steve Prefontaine, whose brash persona dominated track for five years before he was tragically killed at age 24. You

Cranberry harvest time near Bandon

Boardman State Park on the South Coast

Ashland, home of the Shakespeare Festival

can visit Pre's Rock, a memorial at the site of the car accident that killed him, where you'll see a variety of track-related items such as medals, shoes, and race numbers, left behind in his honor. Because of Eugene's historical devotion to track, it's no surprise that the U.S. Olympic Team Trials for Track and Field were held here to great acclaim in 2008.

Besides track, Eugene is also devoted to football, and if you are lucky enough to visit in season, you can take in a Ducks game at Autzen Stadium (come early for tailgating). Be sure to plan ahead, because games are generally sold out.

But there's much more to the University of Oregon than just athletics. Stroll the 295-acre campus, and enjoy the more than 500 varieties of trees that flourish here. You can also visit the Knight Library, the largest in the state, and visit the recently remodeled Jordan Schnitzer Museum of Art. Stop for lunch at the Erb Memorial Union (more often referred to as the EMU) for a taste of student life, or visit one of the bustling cafes along nearby 13th Avenue. And when you've gotten your fill of student life, it's time to experience the rest of what Eugene has to offer.

Downtown, if you visit on the weekend, you can attend Saturday Market, the oldest such market in the country, and purchase items made by local craftspeople. Eugene still has a large population of hippies and devotees of the land, many of whom sell their wares here. Shoppers will also want to stop in at the nearby Fifth Street Public Market, a converted industrial building which now features charming shops and restaurants, with more lining streets nearby. In the mood for some culture? Try the Eugene Symphony, the Eugene Ballet, or the Eugene Opera. Or for some more light-hearted fun, take part in one of the many festivals that the city features—there's the Eugene Celebration, a three-day block party downtown, or the Oregon Bach Festival at the Hult Center for the Performing Arts. The Lane County Fairgrounds, not far out of downtown, hosts a variety of events throughout the year, including the annual Lane County Fair.

Once you tire of city events, there are plenty of outdoor activities to enjoy with the Willamette and McKenzie rivers close at hand. You can fish, boat, or simply take a drive along the McKenzie River and lose yourself in an old-growth forest dream. But don't daydream too long, as we've got many more wonderful destinations ahead. Waving a fond farewell to the city of Eugene, we'll head back up north, with a slight veer to the west to visit Corvallis, the other Willamette Valley college town.

This city of nearly 60,000 is popular with retirees, due to its location, which is near to Portland, as well as the coast and the mountains. Oregon State University is the main employer in town and is known for its programs in engineering, forestry, veterinary medicine, agriculture, and environmental sciences. The 400-acre campus is a beautiful spot for a stroll, but gets crowded on Saturday when the OSU Beavers football team is in town. There are plenty of cultural opportunities associated with the campus and downtown as well. Enjoy concerts and a fine meal afterwards. You may also want to visit the town's farmer's market come spring.

A short distance from Corvallis is the vibrant mid-valley community of Salem, the state's capital. It is no surprise that much of the city revolves around government and politics. Nearly every Oregon schoolchild has visited the Oregon State Capitol, built in 1938 and housing the legislature and the offices of the governor, the secretary of state and the state treasurer. The building is decorated with Depression-era art and also features four types of marble. Don't miss the rotunda, which is adorned with murals depicting Oregon history, as well as scenes of the region's great beauty.

You may also want to visit the Mission Mill Museum while in town. This complex features 14 buildings devoted to history, and visitors can stroll through them all. The largest is the 1889 Thomas Kay Woolen Mill, which was notable in its time for an important reason. It used a water turbine to process wool, and this was the only one west of the Mississippi. The wool industry was a huge part of the economy of the Willamette Valley for a hundred years. But there's far more to the Mission Mill Museum than just a focus on wool. Several other historic structures have been moved to the site, all of them restored. It's fascinating to stroll through these pioneer homes, full of their original furnishings, and get a good idea of how the early settlers in

Morning light at Klamath Lake

Applegate River, Roque River National Forest

Winter at Crater Lake

the area lived. You'll also find a restaurant, gift shop, and gardens to wander through here. History buffs may also be interested in a visit to Historic Deepwood Estate, a restored 1894 Queen Anne Victorian home featuring stained glass and oak woodwork, as well as a 5-acre English garden.

Don't miss Salem's historic downtown, which features shopping, eating, and gallery hopping in beautiful turn-of-the-twentieth-century buildings. At Riverfront Park, you can experience the wonderful sights and sounds of its famous hand-carved Carousel, touted as one of the most beautiful in the country, the enlightening Eco-Ball, outdoor concerts and other community events as you gaze at stunning river vistas. There's also a paddleboat that departs from the park year round.

North of Salem, visit Champoeg State Park for more Oregon history. Here is where Oregon's first government was formed in 1843. The park is located on the Willamette River and features a variety of natural habitats, including forest, field, and wetlands. Not only that, there are several historic structures of interest also. The park's visitor's center is called the Newell House and the Pioneer Mother's Log Cabin is a museum full of exhibits dedicated to the region's history. The Butteville Store located in the park is the state's oldest store. It, too, was opened in 1863 and today is open Friday through Sunday. Once you're done with your history rambles, you can walk or bike trails along the river, picnic, camp, fish or canoe.

One of the best things about the Willamette Valley is simply driving though it. Many flower growers make their homes here, and in the springtime you'll see fields of tulips and iris abloom in all their glory. Wooden Shoe Tulip Farm near Woodburn is one of many that encourages visitors, with tulip festivities in March and April. Nearby Canby is also a good region for flower viewing. This town calls itself "The Garden Spot" and earns its name with a preponderance of nurseries and flower growers. Visit the Flower Farmer or Swan Island Dahlias. The farms will be delighted to take your flower order for your home garden.

Now let's head east on Highway 213 to the beautiful town of Silverton. With a population of just under 8,000, Silverton is small but vibrant, featuring many beautiful Victorian-era homes. Be sure to stop in at the popular Silver Grille Café, just like the locals. Silverton is nestled in a fertile growing area. Nearby you'll find Cooley's Iris Gardens. Of special interest is The Oregon Garden, a 120-acre botanical park featuring 80 acres of specialty gardens. It features the new Moonstone Hotel, and an original Frank Lloyd Wright-designed home. The Garden is a popular spot for weddings, community events and concerts. Take the delightful tram ride and you'll see the Children's Garden, the Conifer Garden, the Pet Friendly Garden, the Lewis and Clark Garden, and the Jackson and Perkins Rose Garden, among many others.

Silverton is also the gateway to Silver Falls State Park, the largest state park in Oregon. Here you'll find 24 miles of hiking trails, 14 miles of horse trails, and 4 miles of bike trails. But the true reason to visit the park is for the waterfalls. The Canyon Trail or Trail of Ten Falls parallels Silver Creek and passes by ten waterfalls, just as the name says. Four of these waterfalls have a spectacular amphitheater-like feature that allows the hiker to actually walk behind the falls.

Leaving the park, let's now head north to the small community of Mt. Angel. You'll want to linger here because of the town and the abbey. The Mount Angel Abbey and Seminary is a thriving community of Benedictine Monks. It is located atop Mount Angel, a 485-foot high butte, and features a library built by Finnish architect Alvar Aalto, and a new bell tower housing one of the largest swinging bells in the Pacific Northwest. In June, the monks offer the Mount Angel Abbey Festival of Art and Wine Tasting, and in July they host a Bach Festival. There is a bookstore and gift shop as well as guest and retreat houses.

The town of Mount Angel is picturesque Bavarian from one end to the other. Absolutely delightful! It has great German food and a life-size Glockenspiel and in September the entire town hosts an everyone's invited Octoberfest celebration. It is huge!

North of Mount Angel is the pretty little town of Woodburn, traditionally a farming center. Now it is home to the Woodburn Company Stores, a busy

Mount Thielsen at Diamond Lake

Historic Wolf Creek Inn

Autumn at Mt. Washington from Big Lake

Mosby Covered Bridge (1920) in Cottage Grove

outlet mall visited by shoppers from all over the region. It is also home to a large community of Russian Orthodox Believers. Some place the size of their community at 10,000 people. This Christian group fled from persecution in Turkey in the 1950s. They are instantly recognizable, as the men have long beards and the woman don brightly colored long skirts and scarves. Their hard-work ethic make them the top farmers in the area.

And now the moment has come for all the wine lovers in attendance, as we're going to head west into Yamhill County, the epicenter of Oregon's burgeoning wine-making operations. Wine country has really come into its own over the past few years, with the area establishing a world reputation as an excellent producer of pinot noirs and chardonnays. Wine lovers from all over flock to the area to visit wineries, taste wine, and partake of special festivals which run all spring, summer, and fall.

The first grapes were planted in the region in the mid-sixties, and lots of people scoffed at the wine pioneers. They aren't scoffing any longer, however, with Oregon wines winning world-wide respect. There are dozens of wineries to visit, ranging in size from large to small. Some wineries charge a modest tasting fee, while others do not. You may be interested in visiting the originator of the Yamhill County wine industry. This is Eyrie Vineyards, founded by David and Diana Lett in 1965. The Letts were the first ones to recognize the potential for growing grapes in the region. The Eyrie Vineyards are located in the Dundee Hills and the winery itself is in McMinnville. Other notable wineries include Sokol-Blosser, Elk Cove, Domaine Serene, and Arborbrook vineyards.

If you are confused by the profusion of wineries to choose from, why not book a wine tour and let them do all the work for you? Several companies offer wine country tours. You can choose to ride in a limousine, town car, or van, and many of the tours will arrange for wineries to serve you lunch as part of your tour. The added benefit is that you can taste as much as you want without worrying about having to drive yourself home.

Your travels in wine country will surely take you to the town of McMinnville, whose charming downtown features businesses housed in historic buildings. Enjoy boutiques, restaurants, and art galleries. You'll also want to stop at the Evergreen Aviation and Space Museum, home to the famous *Spruce Goose* , built by the rakish Howard Hughes during World War II. The museum also features a replica of a 1903 Wright Brothers plane, and many other fascinating exhibits. It is considered one of the finest aviation museums in the country.

Other towns to visit in the area are Dundee, Newberg, Carlton and Amity, to name only a few. You'll find a wide variety of bed and breakfasts, inns, and hotels to accommodate your stay, and plenty of fine dining to accompany the wine. Be sure to book ahead if you're planning to stay over, because accommodations fill up fast, particularly during times of special events and festivals. And Yamhill County is a cheerful place, prone to throw a festival or celebration at the drop of a hat! You might want to experience the UFO Festival and Alien Daze in McMinnville—for true believers only (wink, wink). This event features a parade, an alien pet contest, and vendors selling treats such as "alien ears." Turkey Rama is a popular local event, put on to celebrate the area's once-burgeoning turkey industry and showcasing such events as the Turkey Trot, the Turkey Barbecue, and the Biggest Turkey lip-sync contest. Other festivals and celebrations abound.

Columbia Gorge

We can't stay in wine country forever, tempting as it is (and many a casual visitor has been lured into permanent residence here). There's still lots of Oregon left to explore. Next up on our itinerary is the stunning Columbia Gorge. To get there, we'll pass back through Portland and head east. Views of the Gorge begin quickly after leaving the city, and it is hard to remain unmoved by the grandeur of this 80-mile gorge that forms the border between Washington and Oregon.

The Gorge was formed by glacial floods thousands of years ago, carving a 1,200-mile route for the mighty Columbia River. Above this scenic waterway, canyon-like cliffs rise to heights of 4,000 feet in several places. All along the

South Falls, Silver Falls State Park

The Oregon Garden, Silverton

Oregon's beautiful State Capitol, Salem

river are spectacular views and numerous opportunities for outdoor activities. Kayaking, camping, picnicking, hiking, and river cruises are just some of the options enjoyed by visitors. The more adventurous may enjoy taking a crack at windsurfing. With its high canyon walls, the Gorge creates a perfect tunnel for wind, and because of this it is considered one of the best places in the world to enjoy the sport.

The best place to get your first taste of the Columbia Gorge is just a few miles east of Portland, at Crown Point. Many a first-time visitor has had their jaw drop in awe when they catch a glimpse of the view from this promontory. The building perched atop the cliff is Vista House, which many consider to be the symbol of the Gorge. Built in 1916, the architect of Vista House was Edgar Lazarus, brother to Emma Lazarus, who wrote the famous poem about the Statue of Liberty. Vista House offers a gift shop, museum and interpretive displays and recently underwent a beautiful $3.2 million renovation. It's an excellent place to get your bearings as you begin your Columbia Gorge tour.

This building was constructed at the same time as the Historic Columbia River Gorge Highway, whose narrow roads were for many years the only east-west access through the Gorge. Many visitors today prefer the gentle curves decorated with rock walls of the old road. But allow plenty of time—it is not a quick alternative. You'll see fabulous views galore along the road, however, and also enjoy close up one of the favorite features of the Gorge—its many waterfalls.

The Gorge boasts 77 waterfalls on the Oregon side alone, many of them within a 15-mile area, and they come in all varieties. For the waterfall experts among you, this includes plunge, cascade, horsetail, segmented and more. Many of the waterfalls feature hiking trails, but be aware that these tend to be steep uphill inclines. Most of the falls are easily viewable from parking lot trailheads, many of which feature comfortable picnic areas. You may request a map from the Forest Service to locate the falls, or simply drive along the old Columbia Gorge Highway and you will pass by most of them.

Whichever waterfall you choose to visit, you won't want to miss Multnomah Falls, the grand dame of them all, and at a towering 620 feet,

Historic Deepwood Estate

Salem's Riverfront Carousel

Woodburn Tulip Festival

Laurel Ridge Winery in Yamhill County

The Columbia River, Crown Point and Vista House

Newly restored interior of Vista House

Beautiful Multnomah Falls

Historic Columbia Gorge Hotel

Rooster Rock State Park, in the Gorge

Autumn at Latourell Falls

Punchbowl Falls on Eagle Creek

Opposite page: Beautiful Vine Maple and Mt. Hood at Lost Lake

Winter at Mt. Hood and Timberline Lodge

Lava flow and Huckleberries on Old McKenzie Highway

Mt. Bachelor from Sparks Lake

Autumn on the Deschutes River

Opposite page: Crooked River at Smith Rock State Park

Lake Billy Chinook, west of Culver

Autumn at Elk Lake, South Sister in distance

Spring wheat fields of Sherman County

Cathedral Rock on John Day River

Oregon's most-visited natural attraction. It's easy to see why the falls entice over 2.5 million visitors each year. Towering cliffs and lush forest foliage frame the cascading plunge of water. A paved trail leads to the Benson Bridge, a favorite scenic photo opportunity spot. At the base of the waterfall sits the historic Multnomah Falls Lodge, built in 1925. Here you'll find forest service information, a gift shop, and a restaurant.

After you've meandered along the old highway and visited waterfalls to your heart's content, keep heading east and you'll soon arrive in the picturesque town of Hood River. The town perches above the Columbia and as such offers spectacular views. Stroll along the scenic main boulevard of the town and visit boutiques, cafes, and coffee shops, all while enjoying the amazing views of the river. You'll notice quite a few stores devoted to the sport of windsurfing. Hood River is considered the windsurfing capitol of the world, and this popular sport is one of the main contributors to the city's economy.

But before the windsurfers discovered it, Hood River was always known for its orchards. Pears and apples are grown here, with many of the orchards planted on land with views of Mt. Hood. Farm stands dot the landscape in season, and many Portlanders make it a habit to drive up the Gorge to buy the luscious fruit. (It's a tough job, but somebody has to do it.) And, since we are in the neighborhood, let's journey a bit further east to the city of The Dalles. The many points of interest in The Dalles include the Dalles Dam, the Fort Dalles Museum, and a downtown area rich with historical buildings and murals. Don't miss the Columbia Gorge Discovery Center and Wasco County Historical Museum. Now, let's journey back to see Mt. Hood for ourselves.

Rising to a majestic 11,249 feet, with 12 glaciers, Mt. Hood forms the picturesque backdrop to many Gorge views. (Of course, many Portlanders consider Mt. Hood to be their mountain, as it is usually visible from most locations in the city.) Mt. Hood is the highest peak in Oregon, and while it is officially dormant, it technically could still erupt. Many scientists consider Hood to be the most likely to erupt in the future. Skiers, snowshoers, climbers, and sledders don't pay much attention to this, as they are too busy enjoying all the delights the mountain has to offer.

Mt. Hood presents six ski areas which are Summit, Snow Bunny, Cooper Spur, Ski Bowl, Mt. Hood Meadows, and Timberline Lodge. The latter, a National Historic Landmark, is one of the places you'll want to stop for certain. Located on the south side of the mountain at an elevation of 5,960 feet, Timberline Lodge was built in the 1930s as a Works Progress Administration (WPA) project during the Great Depression. The building is adorned with local stone and timbers, and decorative carved elements throughout. Tourists delight in visiting the lodge, petting the resident St. Bernard dog, and enjoying a meal of top-notch Northwest cuisine. The lodge also offers comfortable and historic accommodations. But skiers return over and over again to Timberline for the skiing. It is the only ski area in North America to offer year-round skiing, and the United States Olympic team has taken advantage of this to train here.

Another favorite ski area is Mt. Hood Meadows, which aficionados claim has some of the best snow in the Northwest. Nestled on the east side of the mountain, where it's not as windy, the resort grooms runs from beginner level to expert.

Central Oregon

Now it is time to head south from Mt. Hood to enjoy the pleasures of central Oregon. You may have already read about the virtues of this region, because many a magazine has focused on it, lavishing praise on the region's recreational activities, historic past, and active urban areas. The first thing you need to understand is that central and eastern Oregon enjoy a vastly different climate than western Oregon. While the west side of the state is famous for its rain, once you get through the Cascade Mountains a far different experience awaits. In fact, many parts of the central region boast 300

Spring at the Painted Hills

Kiger Gorge on Steens Mountain

days of sunshine. The geography that basks in this sunshine is varied—from mountain to lake and stream, from high desert to gorgeous valley. Just like the old saying, "If you don't like the weather, wait 10 minutes," in central Oregon it's, "If you don't like the geography, drive 20 minutes and you'll find something new."

Our first stop on the tour from Mt. Hood to central Oregon is Warm Springs, a sovereign nation within a nation, as it is home to the Warm Springs, Wasco, and Paiute Indian tribes. Relax awhile at Kah-Nee-Ta High Desert Resort and Casino and visit The Museum at Warm Springs to learn more about the history of these proud tribes and their presence in the region.

South of Warm Springs is Smith Rock State Park. A mecca for outdoor enthusiasts who climb, hike, mountain bike, trail run and horse-back ride year-round. Spring and Fall are best here, as temperatures reach 100+ degrees in summer and freezing in the winter months.

Next up is Sisters, a frontier-themed town that is a delight to stroll. Nearby sit Black Butte Ranch, a resort community, the Hoodoo Ski area, and the charming small town of Camp Sherman, located on the Metolius River. And don't miss a visit to the delightful Americana scene you'll find in Redmond. Now it is time to drop into Bend, the county seat and the hub of central Oregon.

This town is growing quickly—from around 50,000 in the 2000 census, to nearly 90,000 in 2008. Why? Perhaps it is because of its location. Bend perches on the eastern edge of the Cascades, along the Deschutes River, right where the pine forest changes into high-desert plateau. This diversity insures a wide variety of outdoor activity—including world-class skiing on nearby Mt. Bachelor.   You'll also find golf, white-water rafting, mountain biking, swimming, hiking, rock climbing and fishing, to name only a few!

Many visitors to the Bend area choose to stay at the Sunriver Resort, 20 minutes south of Bend. It has three championship golf courses, miles of biking trails, and family homes available to rent. But wherever you choose to stay, be sure to schedule time to visit the High Desert Museum. Here you'll learn about the history, culture, wildlife and traditions of the region. Stop into the 1880 Homestead Ranch for a dose of living history, with costumed employees showing you how families lived in pioneer days. You can also get a glimpse of how a turn-of-the-century sawmill operated. And those are just two of the many outdoor exhibits—many more await inside, too.

Eastern Oregon

Alas, it is time to hit the trail again. Our tour of Oregon is soon to draw to a close, but fortunately we still have the vast expanses of eastern Oregon to enjoy. It's so big, it's divided into three areas, and we'll begin in southeast Oregon. You may be surprised that you are still in Oregon when you view the scenery around here, as it is very different from what we've seen so far. Here, you get vast desert vistas, a rugged landscape and broad open spaces. There's far less of an urban presence here, and far more empty land.

Rock lovers will want to visit the John Day Fossil Beds National Monument to see one of the richest fossil beds in the world, including the magical Painted Hills. At the nearby Thomas Condon Paleontology Center you'll learn about the ancient mammals of this region. Further south, the town of Burns in the middle of vast ranching country is also worth a stop. Grab yourself some lunch before heading to the Malheur National Wildlife Refuge. Here is a wetlands of 187,000 acres that is home to 320 species of birds. Join bird watchers from all over the world in checking them out. Next up is the Frenchglen Hotel State Heritage Site. Famous for its home-cooked meals, this 8-room historic hotel is open mid-March to November, and was built in 1924. You can enjoy wide-open spaces and all kinds of recreational activities at the gateway to Steens Mountain. Drive the 59-mile Steens Loop Scenic Tour to get a great idea of this unique region—you'll pass by views of valleys and desert, and see raptors galore.

Now let's head back north again, to northeastern Oregon. This land is varied, too, with tall mountains, deep canyons, plus forests and valleys. We'll begin in La Grande, a hub for the area located in the Grande Ronde Valley between the Blue Mountains and the Wallowa Mountains. It is home

The Pillars of Rome between Rome and Jordan Valley

Wallowa Lake in Northeastern Oregon

to the Eastern Oregon Fire Museum and Eastern Oregon University, which is situated on a hill above the historic downtown and serves ten counties east of the Cascade Mountains.

From La Grande, we'll head into the Wallowas, part of the Wallowa-Whitman National Forest. Drive highway 82 along the beautiful Wallowa River and marvel as the narrow canyons open up into the Wallowa Valley. Framed by the 10,000-foot high Wallowa Mountain Range, you'll immediately see why this part of the state is sometimes called "Little Switzerland" or "The Alps of Oregon." Be sure not to miss the Wallowa Lake Tramway—an outstanding ride and a view to end all views!

A bit of history here: this land was considered sacred territory to the Nez Perce Indians, and in 1855, the US Government took control with the Stevens Treaty. The Nez Perce were to keep their land centered in the Wallowas. It didn't happen, and in 1877, Young Chief Joseph led 800 followers north to within 50 miles of the Canadian border before being caught and sent to live on the reservation. Further on down the road, you can visit Old Chief Joseph's grave near Wallowa Lake in the town that bears his name—Joseph. Joseph is a charming town with a population of 1,000. Not only is it close to Wallowa Lake and the starting point for many outdoor adventures, it is also known as an art town, with many galleries and shops to visit. The town is also home to one of the best-known bronze-casting facilities in the nation, Valley Bronze of Oregon, which utilizes the lost-wax method of creating huge statues. Artists come from all over to have their work cast here, and tours are offered to visitors. Wallowa Lake itself is a gorgeous mountain gem, with high moraines flanking its west and east sides.

Thirty miles east is the fabled Hells Canyon. Designated a National Recreation Area in 1975, it is the deepest river gorge in North America. With access sites for floaters and jet boaters, this part of the Snake River offers fun and adventure for all.

Now, let's double back and head the long way around the mountains to Baker City. When this city calls itself historic, it means it—there are over 110 homes and buildings on the National Historic Register here. You may visit the Adler House Museum for a taste of what an 1880-era home looked like. On the outskirts of Baker City, do not miss the National Historic Oregon Trail Interpretive Center, which brings pioneer days to life. You can see actual trail ruts, and replicas of covered wagons. Indoors, exhibits and living-history performances really give you an idea of what it was like to travel on the Oregon Trail.

As we head back toward Portland to end our journey, we have one more area of eastern Oregon to explore. This is the Columbia River Plateau, home to vast wheat fields, the Blue Mountains, and the city of Pendleton. Once known as a prime example of the Wild West, you can get a glimpse of what those days were like with the Pendleton Underground Tours. Unbelievably, a vast network of tunnels beneath the city afforded a place for a whole other life below, including card rooms, speak easies, meat markets and even an ice cream shop! Another place of note is the Pendleton Woolen Mills, producer of the famed Pendleton blankets, which are still created today.

Drive a few miles outside of town and soon you'll hit the Blue Mountains, a notorious obstacle on the Oregon Trail. Some modern-day drivers may tell you that they are still a fearsome impediment with the hairpin curves that zig and zag up the mountains, and numerous truck escape routes for the drive back down!

From Pendleton, we'll retrace our path down the mighty Columbia and head back into Portland just in time to catch our plane out. Or will we? Many a tourist has come for a visit to this great state and ended up staying. Maybe it's because Oregon has it all—stunning coastlines, towering mountains, vast desert, fertile farmland, old-growth forests, sparkling rivers and placid lakes. And that doesn't even begin to touch on the diversity of its cities and towns. No matter if you decide to come back for another visit or to stay here permanently, one of the varied locales in this state will be just right for you.

Town of Joseph at the base of Wallowa Mountains

Opposite page: Owyhee River Canyon

About the Author
Charlotte Dixon

Once again, when we needed a real professional to do a great text for one of our publications, we turned to Charlotte Dixon. A free-lance journalist living in Portland, Oregon, her great-great grandparents were among the hardy pioneers who followed the Oregon Trail to settle in the West. She has had an affinity for the area all of her life.

With her heritage and extensive traveling in the state she has been able to impart that very important "first hand" knowledge that makes her writings so enjoyable.

She has a degree in journalism from the University of Oregon and she is a past president of Willamette Writers Association. She is kept busy contributing essays and profiles to a variety of local magazines and newspapers, while she continues to work actively to promote the literary arts in the Northwest.

Her association with Beautiful America Publishing Company has been steady. She wrote the text for Beautiful America's MAINE, Beautiful America's WYOMING, and Beautiful America's OREGON COAST.

When she isn't busy at her hobbies of gardening, knitting, reading and hiking, she enjoys traveling with her family throughout the West and especially Oregon.

Photo Credits

RON COOPER - page 49 left and page 49 right

DIANNE DIETRICH LEIS - page 6; page 7 left; page 7 right; page 10; page 11; page 14 left above; page 14 right; page 15 right; page 17; page 20; page 29 left; page 34 right; page 35; page 43 left; page 47; page 50; page 51; page 56; page 59; page 62; page 63; page 73; page 77 and rear cover

MICHAEL DURHAM with Courtesy of Oregon Zoo - page 14 left below

PETER MARBACH - front cover; page 15 left; page 21; page 34 left; page 38 right; page 39; page 42 left; page 46 right; page 53 left; page 53 right; page 54; page 55 left; page 57; page 58; page 60; page 61 left; page 61 right; page 64; page 65; page 68; page 69; page 72 and page 76

JAMIE & JUDY WILD - page 2; page 25; page 29 right and page 80

GEORGE WUERTHNER - page 24; page 28; page 32; page 38 left; page 42 right; page 43 right; page 46 left; page 52 and page 55 right

Snake River in Hells Canyon

Rear Cover: Won't you join us?